Walking Naked Under a Yellow Rain Slicker

Walking Naked Under a Yellow Rain Slicker

Poems by

Deanie Rowan Blank

© 2022 Deanie Rowan Blank. All rights reserved.
This material may not be reproduced in any form, published,
reprinted, recorded, performed, broadcast,
rewritten or redistributed without
the explicit permission of Deanie Rowan Blank.
All such actions are strictly prohibited by law.

Cover design by Shay Culligan
Cover image by Tomas Malik

ISBN: 978-1-63980-203-6

Kelsay Books
502 South 1040 East, A-119
American Fork, Utah 84003
Kelsaybooks.com

In loving memory
of my dearest Joe who paved the path

And for
my beloved Gerry who walked the path with me

To my reader, I advise that you grab the wheel
and drive till you run out of gas—
retreat only for refuel and repair

Acknowledgments

With grateful acknowledgment to the following publications where versions of these poems have appeared, occasionally under different titles:

22nd ITO EN Oi Ocha New Haiku Competition of Japan, English Haiku Division, Commendation Award: "The Mourning Dove Sings"
The Coachella Review: "Cooking Cream of Wheat"
Flying House Press: "Naked Echoes"
The Hartford Courant: "Cooking Cream of Wheat"
In the Shadow of the Sleeping Giant: "Artichoke Heart"
Mediphors: A Literary Journal of the Health Professions: "Post-Menopausal Bone Scan"
The Perch: An Arts and Literary Journal, Yale Program for Recovery and Community Health: "Black Birds Make Me Smile," "Diamond-White Night," "Solace"
Poetica Magazine: "Remember the Children"
Prairie Schooner, special Ireland Edition: "Beneath the Rowan Tree," "Clear West"
Project Muse: "Enchanted," "Clear West"
Whistling Fire, University California Riverside: "Drizzled"

My great gratitude to Stephen C. Behrendt, George Holmes Distinguished University Professor of English, Interim Senior Editor, *Prairie Schooner,* who pulled my poetry from the high sky of submissions to see the light of publication in the Special Ireland issue. I am extraordinarily grateful to Kwame Dawes, Glenna Luschei Endowed Editor-in-Chief of *Prairie Schooner,* who flew me to the University of Nebraska for the Ireland issue launch and for his wise and sincere guidance.

The W.B. Yeats International Summer School, Sligo, Ireland, has been a significant influence on my work over the years. The award of a Pierce Loughran Memorial Scholarship enabled my first experience with the Summer School for which I am eternally grateful. Northern Irish poet Nick Laird led the challenging poetry workshop the first year. I have newfound insights into my writing from Irish poet, Eavan Boland, Professor of English, Stanford University, with whom I have been privileged to study at the Summer School. Special appreciation to Yeats International Summer School supporters and friends: Stella G. Mew, Martin Enright, Maura McTighe, Ian Kennedy, Margaret Raftery.

I am forever thankful to Irish poet, Joan McBreen, for her continuing affirmation. The sage editorial advice of Margaret Mauldon has immeasurably enhanced the clarity of my work. Thank you to my first teacher of poetry, Maria Sassi, Hartford College for Women instructor, who encouraged this poetic journey. My sister and author, Susan Rowan Masters, is my forever literary advisor and support.

Countless thanks to the Hodges University Writers' Workshop colleagues, the Shoreline Cluster Poets group, the Connecticut Poetry Society Writers' group, the Manhattan Writers' group, the Whitney Writers group, the ERATO poetry group, and to those who so freely gave their insight and time, among them: Laura Altshul,

Victor Altshul, Tony Arnold, Joan Blessing, Anthony Castro, Janay Cosner, Mary Davis, Gail DiMaggio, Molly Fisk, Geri Frie, Tony Fusco, Mary Gould, Peter Hunt, Karen Kemetzo, George Kotlan, Gemma Mathewson, Harold Obstler, Rudy Sturk, and my singular pen and chat pal Joan Wexler.

Of course, this life and these poems would not have been possible without the love, support, and encouragement of family including, Nancy and Roy Bernhardt, Gerry Blank, Michael Blank and Marlene Eisenberg, Robert and Joan Blank, Naomi Blank, Evi Gilles, Hal and Karen Herdy, Joe LaPlante, Eve LaPlante and David Dorfman, Chuck Masters, Ted Masters, Jon Masters, Uwe and Karin Marhenke, Ruth and Bill Piazza, Diana Raffman, Nancy Raffman, Art and Suzanne Sadler, Ursula and Bob Spiegel. Also, Grands: Charlotte, Chris, Clara, Dawn, Elijah, Fabian, Isaac, Jeff, Julius, Lilo, Lisa, Lorenz, Philip, Rose, and Great grands, Jack, Kristina, Tejasvin, Vishal, Vivek.

And friends including, Ilana and Norman Adler, Ed Bezzo, Cele and Frank Casa, Judy and Allen Cullison, Elizabeth and Norman Foxman, Kathleen Hayes, Adrienne Marks, Pamela and Patrick McIntyre, Sharon McIntyre, Jane Nolan, Don and Irene Pomerantz, Ann P. Steele, Jane Schell, Judy Thompson.

A Coat
—William Butler Yeats

I made my song a coat
Covered with embroideries
Out of old mythologies
From heel to throat;
But the fools caught it,
Wore it in the world's eyes
As though they'd wrought it.
Song, let them take it
For there's more enterprise
In walking naked.

Contents

I. The Pulse of Grief

The Dead of Night	19
Solace Echoes	20
The Gift of Grief	21
Charlotte's Web	22
Black Birds Make Me Smile	23
Love Notes	24
Audacious Decisions	40
Diamond White Night	42
Fire of Creation	44

II. The Impulse of Joy

Dust to Dust	47
Joy and the Ache of Being	48
Paris Diptych	50
Drizzled	53
Remember the Children	55
Exotic Beauties	56
Circe Survives	58
Post-Menopausal Bone Scan	59
Fugue for the M.R.I. Virgin—Before Earphones	60
True Beauty	61
Sicilian Ceremony	62
Beneath the Rowan Tree	65
Cooking Cream of Wheat	66
Hummingbird	67
Dulcet Laughter	68
My Cousin Harmonia	69
Other Mother	70
Naked Echoes	71
When You Don't See What's in Front of You	87

The Greek Ring	88
Something about Sligo	89
Favors from Fierce Seas	90
Clear West	91

III. The Spur to Persist and Thrive

For My Husband in Equatorial Africa	95
Time Now	96
What's the Point?	97
What's Next	98
Cadences	99
The Men I Married	100

IV. My Menagerie

Imperial Grace	103
Backyard Dominion	104
Food for Thought	105
My New Live-In Pal	107
A Fish Empathy Project?	109
The Mourning Dove	110
Cost of Carnage	111
Unseen Peril	112
The Raven Reveals	113
Ecstasy	115

I. The Pulse of Grief

. . . As life goes on we discover that certain thoughts sustain us in defeat, or give us victory, whether over ourselves or others, and it is these thoughts, tested by passion, that we call convictions . . . We begin to live when we have conceived life as tragedy.
   —William Butler Yeats, *Four Years: 1887–1891*

The Final Phase . . . is vital; it is a closure, yet it is also a moment of arrival, and therefore a possible new beginning.
   —Mary Oliver, *Winter Hours*

The Dead of Night

She swirled the honey-toned nectar,
leaned closer, and listened to chosen laments—
lonesome Hank Williams cried—once more
                she poured.

Nascent leaves visible in the window
when he last sat in that chair. Its newsprint-
stained arms, evidence of his thirst for words.
                The *Times* piled high, never again . . .

She poured. A tide of liquid rose
with her tears. Other lyrics surged in waves . . .
If I were a bluebird, I'd soar . . .
                If I were a bluebird . . .

Finally, held in Verdi's embrace, the cognac infusion flowed.
At dawn, she climbed the stairs, breathed in a white cloud
of shirts in his closet
                as morning magpies roused.

The *E`dessa!* duet ended. She fell between cherry posts
of their bed. Still his scent clung to the down of pillows.
Her temples throbbed as a sparrow
                hit hard against the windowpane.

Solace Echoes

Sorrow's cold night confronts
dawn's flaming yawn

sunrise glides to gold-blue sky
frames clouds set to clear

by dusk

frigid night returns, to retreat
once more into day's light

dims to evening's new dark
and full moon's rising

mellow glow.

The Gift of Grief

The dawn of death
        strains endurance
The dusk of death
        more fairly received

I do not damn
        the midnight of death
For it is the dark portion
        of a fully lighted day

Charlotte's Web

Charlotte, with superior wit, fought for Wilbur,
the weakest of the farrow. She was a vital
advocate for his survival from a cruel fate.
Then, exhausted, and alone,

she died. You may think this mad,
but Charlotte's story evokes my sorrow
after I found my husband, the note,
the emptied Nembutal bottle.

A professor of law, he fought
to fix firmly basic rights—
especially every one's right to live
and die with dignity.

His body spent by Parkinson's,
exhausted and alone, he acted
finally, and to shield me—
no one,
no one
was with him
when he died.

Black Birds Make Me Smile

Early in our courtship, he told of fondness
for these black-clad creatures. The contrariety

of black birds attracted him. He saw their beauty,
admired their wily ways, enjoyed their notoriety.

Mythic winged things of ill omen. Raucous
scavenging strumpets, clever, not simply black,

iridescent as an oil slick in sun—silver, green, gold,
blue. When light dims ravens turn velvet ebony hue.

Crows' caws mimic sounds
of a new babe's babble.

He was a bit of a rascal himself.
A bowtie kind of guy with flair

for demonic wit. Students, colleagues
awed by his art—Socratic irony.

So, no grand paradox, his favored
refrains, folk lyrics—*If I were*

a blackbird I'd leave all the sorrow
behind. When the tocsin of mortal disease

tolled—knowing the denouement, he chose
to close the cover of the tome before him.

Love Notes

1. Twenty-Seven Years After

Here it is, Independence Day, so I consider
your liberation. I've been thinking of writing
about your decision and our years together.
Tonight, I began reading my notes to you
since then. My memories move like expanding clouds
and sheered or shadowed contrails as I revisit them.
I see my long-ago Sahara Desert has evolved
into an oasis of both flora and weeds, hemlocks
that topple in storms as well as deep-rooted oaks.

You, a Bronze Star veteran, professor,
noted author, athletic and accomplished actor.
What an odyssey—you, like Theseus, entangled
in a tragic web, a destiny from which there was no
escape, until you launched the silken thread
of your solution.

2. One Year After

The candle in the brass holder burns
as it has from time to time after you left.
Tonight, a year since you reached your coda
as if in a Mahler's Ninth Symphony adagio.
Yesterday I sat on your bench—the one I chose
to honor you—under the small overhanging birch.
It faces the new library. Pink Astilbes and white Hostas
cluster along the corner of the classroom building
to my left. Even with nearby air-conditioners,
the sound was melancholy, restful. A soft breeze
brushed my cheek—I like to think it was your caress.
I think of how you once mused, "This is a Greek tragedy."
Life now is different, no high peaks and deep valleys,
rather a gentle plateau cut by an occasional canyon.

3. Seven Years After

Do you know you have three beautiful granddaughters?
Sharon is a wonderful mother. In our early married
years, when you had so little privilege over Sharon's care,
there was your tenacity to be present for Sharon,
three-years-old when you divorced, ten when we met.

Sharon and I are careful not to crack the crystal
between us. We were both hurting and angry
after you died. She had just lost her dad.
Only two months later, I was with my dying father.
Sharon was to be married in two days, so I left him.
My dad died the next day—my god, what a brutal
concurrence. Sharon, beautiful in a simple white dress,
the bouquet of white roses. Yet, I could not
shake my sorrow to share her joy.

I trust Sharon, and I will see through the dust
of this graveled road, that your grandchildren
will come to know you through my eyes.
So, what is it I loved about you? Your big,
handsome head filled with smarts, how you
understood this world, how I began to appreciate
opera with you. I loved your splendid tennis thighs,
your wit, and your smile. I loved your ability to make
everyone feel at ease, important, special—especially me,
and your patience—especially with me. I honor and grieve
your heroic effort to live and to die a whole man.

I will never forget your unfailing encouragement of my goals,
your earnest advice and support—professional and otherwise.
Lucky me—two true loves. I believe you'd be pleased to learn,
four years after your death, Tim and I married. He is also
incredibly generous regarding my quest as a poet.

There's more: how you finished the Sunday Times Crossword
in ink, the way you got *New York Times* newsprint on everything,
the way your shirts were burned with cigar ashes
before you quit smoking; of course, your poker nights
in the basement with your cigar-smoking pals.
You told me how your mother paid for her Rockport home
with Poker winnings you sent back during your army air force
days in France. I recall learning one of your responsibilities
as a French interpreter included finding fine wine for the officers.

The depth of your humility was not fully appreciated
by me until you were gone, when your good friend Dan told,
at your memorial service, of your courage, you a young law
professor spoke on the floor of the state legislature
for women's rights to abortion, long before it had public
support. I think now of your answer when I once asked
how you came to be on NARAL's mailing list. You said only
something about having supported them in the past.

You were always ahead of the curve
on matters of tolerance, inclusion.
And I loved how you stayed behind the curve
wearing your outdated fashion of self-tied bowties.

4. Eight Years After

It's another year since my last note and the anniversary
of your death is with me. Sharon has asked about you
and our early years together. I've shared some,
before Parkinson's was your jailer in the shadows.
Not the anxiety you felt becoming a spectacle,
the humiliation of a prisoner in a wheelchair
as Parkinson's brutalized your blameless body.

I've been remembering the spring, before our June
wedding, when your psychiatrist recommended a limited
course of electroshock therapy since your depression
just wasn't lifting. You insisted I still attend my planned
Chicago business trip. From the beginning, I understood
that depressive dips were a part of you. As a mental health
clinician, I didn't question the treatment. We spoke a lot
by phone and when I returned you were already home,
and much improved. In fact, later that month you acted
in another play. Our friends gave us an engagement party
at the end of May. I remember that fall driving home
on the daily half-hour trip back, singing how much I loved
being married to you, how much I cherished the thought
that you, my husband, and I would soon be home together.

There was the night I stormed out in anger that fall—
I don't recall the reason, but I assumed you would
come after me, like the story my mom told of my dad
running after her once when they'd argued. You didn't.
You didn't even make your usual "come to bed" bidding
from my effort to sleep on the sofa. That was the last
of my silly Prima Donna scenes. Oh, how I regret
the time I ran out on you several years later—when the tank
you held onto for support tore from the wall. At that moment,

the gushing water seemed to drown my endurance. I raced
into the dark, leaving you there. As I fled, I wished
to be attacked, so I could fight back. It seemed hours
before I returned from my murderous rage,
found you on hands and knees wiping up the water.
You said it was okay, forgave me.

Remember The Finger? There it is, standing
in the right rear corner of my desk, the little
clutched fist with the middle finger pointing straight up.
The wood-carved figurine was in the sales case
of the touristy Polynesian Restaurant near the Loop.
I just couldn't resist this gift to you on my return
from another Chicago trip. You were the one to teach me
the fun of saying "fuck" in certain circumstances—
me, who broke up with my first college boyfriend
for the same offense. Fortunately, Tim, who never swears,
remains affable midst my bawdy banter.

I think of your depression our third married year.
We managed to climb out of that valley, soon after
reached a new peak as you planned our time in Italy
where friends lived, and in Greece where we found
my modest golden Greek ring. Then you, back to teaching,
writing. Me, to directing, consulting, and both of us,
to bridge, tennis, parties, concerts. Best of all,
you taught this unfledged upstate-grown gal how
to navigate Manhattan. Not to mention the London trip,
cocktails and talk of the local theater scene, with your friend's
friend, Lady Fermoy, Lady-in-Waiting to the Queen Mother.
We met up with Sharon who introduced us to her Ireland
where she was studying. We three took off for France.
I'll always remember our night at the Paris Opera.

We had a magnificent view, not of the stage,
but being top of the top balcony, we could nearly
touch the glorious Chagall ceiling.

While we still lived in the high-rise apartment,
your gait began to change, you were slower to maneuver.
I think of Sharon's call down to you from our balcony,
"Dad, you're limping." I came to understand your depressions,
when the Parkinson's diagnosis was finally made. By then,
Sharon spent summers with us, worked at the local
garden center to supplement her college allowance.
We were a family.

Remember when you took to your bed
after we signed the contract for our Blue Ridge Lane
home? You compared your mood then, to the character
in the Russian novel you were reading, wittily called it
your *Oblomov* days. It became our personal phrase
for your periodic melancholy. How I wish I'd kept notes
of your other amusing idioms, your aphorisms,
to meliorate shadowed hours.

Was that near the time I had the TIA? It began
with a temporary numbness in a foot one-night
while developing photos in the basement. Days later
I had a piercing unrelenting headache that lasted hours.
The next day, after a staff meeting, all of a sudden
I couldn't speak or move. Except for some residual
amnesia, I recovered. Told to stop birth control—
no pregnancies followed, so my fibroids
were useful after all.

How well you did on the Parkinson's meds
in the beginning. Remember the summer we spent
with the Marshals sailing the St. Lawrence Seaway
on those two clunky but comfortable rented houseboats?
We'd dock near one another every night. Mornings
we'd join on one or the other deck for breakfast,
evenings for drinks before dinner. I think of that night
we docked outside a port and woke in astonished
alarm at how close we were to that freighter.
From then on we docked beside handsome
sailing yachts in safe harbors.

As I was saying, you responded well to the meds
until your stroke—it was a summer during
our Truro, Cape Cod vacation. It nearly destroyed
your power with words. I began writing then, a poem
about that experience—I mention our return
the next summer, your speech still improving,
your comment as I drove—that you'd be
the "nag-i-vator." I use it now with Tim.

Six months of recovery, then you planned
to get back to your law students the next semester.
Instead, we skidded on ice into the veering semi
on our return from Christmas holidays with my folks.
After your broken-ribbed week in the hospital, I think
of your daily visits, reading *The Women of Anna Purna*
to me during my second month of inpatient care.
Two more months before I was back in my office
on two crutches, then one, then a cane finally,
on my own. We were some pair, weren't we?

In our second decade, Parkinson's became paramount
in our lives. We began the daily downward cascade.
That day, in the Ivoryton Playhouse enjoying a summer
matinee musical, at intermission you could not move,
could not get out of your seat without the usher's help.
You never had the shaking, instead, the disease
caused you to freeze. That stylish beard was a good
solution as your smile began to fade, your splendid face
became less and less animated. We never knew
at what moment the medication would stop working.
There you'd be, trapped in the car, in the bath—
remember how our friends joked
we might refill the tub,
float you out?

Was it our fifteenth year—the afternoon you fell
on the tennis court signaled something more devastating.
Activity stimulated the dopamine in your Parkinson's brain,
so until then, tennis was something you still enjoyed.
When you said, never again to tennis, I saw you become
desperate over mounting physical losses, you worried
you were not up to your scholarly self.
There was an overdose—just when was that?
Not getting the timeline straight is like driving
in the dark with low beams. You weren't hospitalized
but your recovery took days. I didn't intend to tell Sharon
when she phoned and you couldn't answer. I did not expect
to tell her why. She asked about you, at my hesitation
she insisted on knowing what was wrong.
I broke. Sharon came to help nurse you. It was
a crushing experience for her.

Oh my, the lights of recollection just switched
to high-beam, I remember now that Sharon and I
took a walk together that time. During the walk
Sharon suggested we might become closer one day,
if, or when you died. Stunned, I replied, "I don't know."
Perhaps that's what Sharon meant, some months after
you died when she said: "You should have protected me."—
I never asked what more she wanted, what more
she needed. I fear now it may be too late for such a talk.

5. Ten Years After

Two years since I last wrote to you and ten years
from that night I found you, the emptied prescription
bottles, the typewritten notes about my being a good wife,
where to find important papers, whom to consult
for advice and help.

Once you had the means to end your life you calmed,
seemed able to bear on . . . I wasn't ready. Were you trying
to protect me, to protect Sharon, by not saying when
you intended to act, assuring we would not be with you?
Just before I left that evening you were busy helping
our neighbor's daughter phone a vet to treat the injured
bird she'd just found in the road—so typical of you.
Why was I not alert to the St. Lawrence freighter
about to bear down on us?

Good news, a grandbaby boy just born
to Sharon and Mark. How about that? Perhaps
my mom told you—she died five years after you—
assuming you are both in the same vicinity.
Look out for my dad who should be nearby.
He died two months after you. My sweet Sam—
your not-so-favorite Frenchie—suffered
a brain tumor about the same time, had to be put down.
No question that was my multiple whip-lash year.

Tim was the only new person Mom remembered
in her last years. I believe she knew he would be good
to me—she loved him as she loved you, because of that.
I think you would approve of Tim, his sense of humor,
differs from your grand wit, Tim's more laid back, pertinent,

he can pull a good joke or therapeutic story from his magnificent
medical memory. We met about two years after you died, married
two years later. Soon after, I inadvertently called him
by your name, and Tim responded to my apologetic concern,
"That's okay; he sounds like a person I'd have liked to know."
Tim's been a big help with Sharon, especially when periods
were still awkward between us. Tim advised when Sharon
asked for a loan to help with their new home,
"Money should be given with a warm hand." So I decided
no loan, a gift then, rather than to wait till I was dead
and my hand cold. Yes, I believe you'd like Tim.

You always said you wanted no special memorial or burial
other than cremation. I hope you're not annoyed with me
for the bench—it's a good solid bench of the same quarried
granite as the Gothic library, and other campus buildings,
and it's a pleasant place to be. When students are about,
it is full of life. I'm told they enjoy sitting here to think,
to talk. Perhaps some of them take note of the inscriptions:
Teacher - Colleague - Friend. Sharon and I agreed
you'd prefer "teacher" to "professor."

I'm thinking of when we first met. Me in a new state,
a new job, beginning to find and develop new friends.
I met Carol at the Unitarian Meet and Greet. She invited
me to join her for a play in which you were performing.
When you asked us to join you and your date for coffee
after the performance, I didn't give any thought
to seeing you again. Your call a couple of nights later
was a surprise. My response was a bit short, as my date
and I were having martinis before dinner.
It wasn't till the next day I thought about my rather
abrupt dismissal of your invitation. I actually rummaged

through the wastebasket to find the Playbill
of your performance so I might have your last name
and call to apologize—something I ordinarily
wouldn't do. It was a wise move on my part
since you said you would not have called again.

Two dates later we sat across from one another
in my living room talking about how much
we enjoyed being together and no matter what happened
we thought we might always be friends. By the end
of the night, we were more than friends.
That was in the spring. By fall you mentioned
you'd like to come with me when you learned
I was having Thanksgiving with my family,
nine hours from here. I knew then you were hooked—
you, however, needed more time to catch on.
By Christmas, I told you I was planning a trip
to Europe and wanted you to join me,
but only if we were married.
We had no question about our love, only
you were concerned you were still having
depressive periods, and you did not wish
to have more children—your first responsibility
was to Sharon. Once you realized I could handle this,
we set the wedding date. Sharon, then a charming
twelve-year-old flower child added to our wedding joy.

6. Sixteen Years After

Sorry, Darling, I've been so long keeping you up to date.
Since Matt and I now have a winter home in Naples,
and a place on the Long Island shore (remember
how we almost bought that land in Truro?),
as well as my poetry. . . . I don't have much time
but wanted to tell you Sharon is somehow managing
with three dynamic girls and a spirited boy
as well as her writing—she's a successful author,
two books so far. Can you imagine, you have four grandchildren!
A few years back, Sharon asked if it was OK for the kids to think
of Matt as their grandfather since they can never touch you.
Of course, he was delighted to include them with his six living
grandchildren in the states and three in Europe, so all together
now there are thirteen—who would have conceived of me,
who cannot conceive, of having all these grand
children to love? More later.

7. Twenty-two Years After

Sharon and I are doing well together these days.
The two older girls are communicating via e-mail with me.
I am so pleased about this. Oh, yes, e-mail is done
between computers. It became common
about five years after you died.

It's been six years since my last note to you.
I've made it eight years beyond your so young sixty-seven.
Just now, as I review this note, my dad comes to mind—
how he loved Hank Williams' sad song, *I'm so Lonesome
I Could Cry*." I'm not lonesome, but I am crying.

I'll try to get back soon but am tired,
must get to bed. No longer do I catch
your "come to bed" call to me each night.

My Last Note

There's been much I've told you these past years
about Sharon, about my thoughts, my feelings,
a bit about Matt—we celebrated our twenty-second
anniversary this last December. You and I had barely
reached our twentieth before you chose to die.
Our twenty-fated married years were like climbing
a steep staircase, weren't they? We made it to the top,
fell back to a landing, caught a breath, slipped back down
a stair or more.

Who'd have thought a girl from a small
town that had lost its luster, after the Great War,
would find such a dazzling, raffish love. Your presence
enhanced all who loved you. Your courage was great,
aware you were dying in your own life, that merely
being present in this world was not sufficient for being
present to yourself. I think of your amusing, often-quipped
insistent mantra during our years together,
"a man's got to do what a man's got to do."
That is just what you did.

Love

Audacious Decisions

One must imagine Sisyphus happy.
—Albert Camus, Myth of Sisyphus

I.

The sun is out
                                        like a light.

The rain is steady at present,
though dormant; torrents are forecast.
Winds rage like a rattled bull.
I feel a flash flood on the way.
Yet, in blackest hours,
                                        stellar
night skies become
                                        brilliant

just as sun-clouded days spark
delight at the sight of shadowed vistas.
Should dark days stay and
                                        vitality

forever fade, with no prospect of sun's
shadows restored—grateful for life's joys,
I will not despair sunlight's fading.
I embrace this time, savor
the Pinot Noir as it leaves my lips,
passes over my palate to the finish.

II.

I aim to kill
                                        time.

Should dark days stay and
                                        lucidity
                                        forever fade

with no prospect of sun's shadows
relished—grateful for past joys,
I will not despair sunlight's passing.
I will choose a good death—
                                        to leave this *mortal*
                                        coil with dignity

of vivid bliss. I will not
assume a smiling Sisyphus.

Diamond White Night

I have had a most rare vision. I have had a dream past the wit of man to say what dream it was.
—William Shakespeare, *A Midsummer Night's Dream,* Act 4, Scene 1

1.

The world was mine, filled with zest and rapture—
cool Manhattan, white Athens, marbled Rome.
Unknowing then of near disaster,
elusive as reflections in slick chrome.
In prime, my love met life's volleys leaping.
So subtle the symptoms, nothing feared.
Unaware the cistern was seeping,
eroding life, death by degrees appeared.
To think of the future, I did not dare.
Vital nerve nexuses would evaporate—
every day fraught with new nightmares.
Losses grieved, I battled to compensate.
No longer the fine athlete full of grace.
Gone, whimsy and laughter from his fine face.

2.

When relentless disease quashed his spirit
and there was no possible means of repair,
he chose the kindest release and took it—
freed himself from pain, endless despair.
My heart turned empty as a barren womb.
My future forsaken, chances taken,
it did not matter that I faced my doom.
Yet in a rare dream, I did awaken.
My fear now is, I cannot create
a poem with the wisdom to define

or with a master's palette to relate
the exquisite dream that once was mine.
I craved to stay, desired no release;
still, my waking brought a reclaimed peace.

3.

To bring forth the splendor is my goal.
I ascended on currents of lambent light
from the moonless cavity of my soul.
And I was not alone on this grand flight.
Oh, the bliss to feel his presence once more—
a gift of ecstasy sublime.
May I never reach another shore
but hold fast my moment of perfect time.
Where joy was lost, mere memories must suffice.
Behind me, the frosted fiery twilight
mounted with wings, high above black ice.
I flew to the eye of diamond-white night,
saw him, free, sleek as a blackbird, soar
toward a new dawn. I awoke to explore.

Fire of Creation

by sparks of coition—
whether love or lust—kindled
in a cradle of coals, surges to flames
that grow tall, burn with warmth, joy,
celebration, while the heat of breath grows
promises. In its prime, the fire will burn, brightest
of celestial bodies, red as the fiery eye of Aldebaran
to the blue-white star of Vega. When the orange glow of inner
space enlightens fire's heart, it becomes self-sustaining.

No longer is close tending vital. Yet, for the fire to survive
as energetic, forceful, the pulse of fuel—joy, love,
kinship, valued as a source of caring—is once
more called upon. *Eyes like a flame of fire*
tell the blaze has reached pledged
potential. When at some time
in every fire, inner flame
fades, warm fellowship
rekindles spirit.

Memories—the tender look
in a beloved's eyes—sustain, while
flames dim to glowing embers, settle
as ashes, to refresh this fertile earth once more.

II. The Impulse of Joy

. . . humor . . . has its value, I think. The hard and sordid things of life are too hard and too sordid and too cruel for us to know and touch them year after year without some mitigating influence, some kindly veil to draw over them, from time to time, to blur the craggy outlines, and make the thorns less sharp and the cruelties less malignant.
　　　—Mark Twain, "A Humorist's Confession"

Dust to Dust

I know I will die.
I do not know what happens
between now and then.

So
for now, I find joy
in found treasures—
beach-stones, scarred,
smoothed by sand-filled
waves. I sing for myself,
often obliviously. I see
bees and butterflies. I hear
hummingbirds and hawks. I watch
leaves waltz in wind, drip in rain. I smell
sweet peas and the sugar breath of babies. I feel
my crash-repaired knee—
the ache, a reminder
of my good fortune
to be walking on it.

I create sculptures
from the muddy
dust of storms.

Joy and the Ache of Being

on listening to Dvorak's String Quintet in G major, Op 77

This quintet draws me
to the rare drama of a double bass
that reveals the full scheme of life,
for it is not only violins, cellos, and violas
that make exquisite chamber music. Add a big
bassist, from Charles Mingus to Koussevitzky,
and you've got cliffhanging, lion taming,
dark nights, neon lights, and flaming skies.

The brisk, vigorous first movement
evolves into a lighthearted fire of life,
and I am fueled with desire, to grasp
the future with gratitude and sufferance
for a brim-filled platter—crème brûlée,
sour lemons, Honeycrisp apples, sea salt,
thyme, ginger, pears, pepper,
pomegranate, and more.

In the second movement, I find irresistible
the duality of life's gentle touches and hard
rock stumbles—sensible sounds that reflect
fundamental lessons in survival.

As the slower third movement opens, always,
I feel loss of those I've loved—they no longer
hold me, tease me, annoy me, play with me.
I know they loved me—there can be no greater
gift than this remembrance. Always,
a bittersweet mist of tears appears; always
on listening to these lyrical tones.

Finally, I am comforted by the impassioned
fourth movement. The first violin soars
to celebrate life richly lived, like breaking
a fortune cookie and finding my fortune:
"Open another fortune cookie."

Paris Diptych

I. In the Middle of the Marais, 1992

Delayed at De Gaulle until baggage
of someone not on board is located.
From the plane's port, I saw two black
cases carried away. Later, headed home
over night Atlantic, I learned the bags
belonged to a woman newly arrived
from Istanbul. It was the last time

I saw Paris. While stabs of his death
dulled in the final days of earth's full turn,
I had spun out of orbit—reckless sex
no longer my opiate.

These new weeks in Paris,
to slow down, clear the haze
in my head. A friend knew a flat
I could afford. There it was: disarming,
old world, with stained facade, four flights up
in the middle of the Marais—

steps from Ile St-Louis, Notre-Dame,
the Picasso Museum nearly in my backyard,
a short walk to the Louvre. The best times,
this time, were not with the cathedrals
but with Sainte-Chapelle, the early
enchanting chapel built for only the King
and his crew. Nor were most pleasurable
moments with Manet and Monet.
It was the Marais itself—

mainly the little grey cat with a pink collar.
Each morning she'd peer hesitantly,
from the building across the way,

then climb out the window,
sit on the roof near the chimney,
watch workmen gentrify the quarter
in the street below. She'd hop about
the slate roof, chase flying insects,
imagined demons. Before the radiant
stone scorched her paws, the little minou
would scoot back in, nearly knocking
daily fresh-cut daises.

Like a feline sprung
off sun-baked slabs,
I stilled, stretched,
catnapped
to engine
hums.

II. Return to Paris, 2010

There was an edge in my eagerness
to return where raw grief remained
embraced in the Marais
two decades away.

I failed to pinpoint the walkup that overlooked grey rooftops
but fixed where the haute couture shop had swallowed
my modest café. Then, as a no-iron shirt sheds wrinkles,
I straightened out. Freed of a need to find again
the Mariage Frères tea house, or walk to the Île Saint-Louis
in search of past haunts.

I slipped from that curious comfort—
the pull of sorrow.

A store of fresh Marais memories grew
like fine rooms added to a family home.
Holding tight to another love's hand, we saw
a wee crêperie, nearly hidden on the Rue de la Mule.
We sat on crowded stools, spoke of our first shared crêpes—
fromage, sucre de beurre—in the old quarter of Genève.

Another day, on Monet's pantry shelf, in Giverny,
I was drawn to the petite white porcelain feline,
adorned in a many-colored gilded bow,
asleep on a slight pink pillow.

Drizzled

over romaine
greens. I wonder
at the pleasure
these pungent
fungi bring—
gold in a chef's pan.
White truffle oil,
my preference,
more peppery
than the black.
Makes sense—
being part Sicilian—
that the robust Italian
whites appeal more
than the tamer ebon
French ones.
All sub-rosa
root-clinging
symbiotic fruiting
tubers—a cabal
of crafty warty walnuts.
Beware the poisonous
false ones. A bit of
truffle oil in brash
hands can be
dreadful excess. Know
the supreme risk—
a snuffling sow
with a bent
for ravenous love
when that special
pheromone flares. Still,
it's truffles' hidden
nature that intrigues—
concealed

         like the echoed
            treasure of my
           memories,
         my musings,
        secrets I let
        drizzle
           in
            my
           mind.

Remember the Children

The black opal, iridescent with fire blue, gold, green
and red, leaped to bright light of the seven-forty-seven's coach
as we hurled from Ben Gurion to JFK.

Australian stone crafted into the jeweled gold and silver
ring, near the Mediterranean port town, Akko—
where proof of peace and war survives

3000 years BCE to this time. Now, young soldiers gather
in another courtyard—all are obliged to know Yad Vashem.
Each with his or her rifle. Some slung across stalwart

backs, others carried in arms, as a parent holds a babe.
From blistering Jerusalem's noonday sun into blind
dark of the daunting Children's Memorial, I descended

the spiral path, encircled by countless reflected stars, resonant
with endless recitation—name, age, place of each child's
murder. One million and one half-million more stolen

from the planet's future. A semi-automatic barrel brushed by
my arm in the blackness . . . The plane banked. I put the paperback
down on the tray table, once more admired the brilliant gem . . .

recalled an earlier treasure—the Sky King shine-in-the-dark
secret compartment ring. I'd slip to sleep in the glow
from that simple prize. Hushed sounds of soon-to-be

golden oldies drifted over my childhood bed. Mother and Dad
resting from laundry, mowing, knowing I was safe beneath
the sweet-scented white sheets just down from a day in the sun.

In the dimmed cabin,
I remembered the children.

Exotic Beauties

"What is it?" The checkout kid tries to key
the non-scannable item into the register.
I hold it in my palm, gently bear down. Its flesh
presses in with my thumb indentation, bounces
back, confirming it is ready. I note the dimple
at the blossom end. Believing folk wisdom
that round dimples have more seeds, are less
meaty, I've selected two, a male oval-dimpled
one, and a spheric she-plant as well, I take care—
mindful aubergines are easily bruised.

"It's a vegetable," my response. I doubt he cared
it was a fruit, eaten as a vegetable. Found
in eighth century India, introduced by Arabs
to Spain, then to Africa by Persians. Nor would he
fix on its kin: tomato, potato, sweet pepper,
Jerusalem cherry, ornamental petunia, tobacco,
and horse nettle. The teen's itch for illumination
might have peaked had I really said, "You hold
a succulent, gently ripened female of the species;
touch her tenderly."

...

Aubergine, a title to provide romance.
Yet, caution; wear gloves when harvesting
for unseen prickly thorns on the stem protect.

I think of Matisse when he finished *Interior
with Eggplant;* so too, Peale's *Still Life:
Balsam Apple and Vegetables.* Of course,
The Eggplant Georgia O'Keefe painted
moves me to other appetites.

As demanding fussy divas, I consider
the careful attention they command.
Assure all danger of frost is past. Harvest
before age sets in; for, like elders, they turn
dull-skinned, brownish, spongy, seedy,
cold-sensitive, sometimes bitter.

Usually baked, grilled, sautéed, sliced,
cut into strips, cubed, or stuffed. Unfit
as raw. Prepare with provolone, pecorino,
pancetta, pesto, or pasta, perhaps a simple Baba
Ghanoush on pita. A wallflower if alone. Veiled
in herb and spice perfumes, becomes a dazzling
cabaret star or sultry lounge singer. I prepare
them with garlic and olive oil that rushes in
as air pushes out of cells to replace all water
in the plants. A dieter's dream, nirvana
for vegetarians—no hacked bloody carcass.
Simply sublime invitation to a banquet.
I fancy the feast to follow.

Circe Survives

I shriek, *The phoebes are back!*
thrilled at their fervent nesting
as if I were the six-year-old
I no longer am, or when my
sixteen-year-old self raced
at a ponytail gallop,
all applesauce smiles
and hot tin-roof hormones.

Now I look around'
does anyone notice
when my very center throbs
at the thought of his tennis-
tight thighs? Do they have
any notion of what Circe survives
in the skin of this sexagenarian?

Post-Menopausal Bone Scan

Her pelvis perfectly aligned, arms hugged
to hips. She lay on slab as the scanner

had its way with her. This broad's bones weren't
so bad, but one day she'd turn up her toes.

Hence, lying there she began to plan her
own memorial. Bawdy bones roasted,

hedonistic habits toasted, a soupçon
of quips in the wake of something sober.

Violetta's *Ah! Gran Dio!* duet, a grand
dénouement. Cindered remains scattered

beneath a beech tree on a breezy
blooming day. And a crusty crony

dodging bone dust might be heard to say,
"Can't deny—she was a great piece of ash."

Fugue for the M.R.I. Virgin—Before Earphones

Disrobe. The noises
remind me of Philip Glass's
solo piano, *Mad Rush,* in echo
chamber   chamber   chamber.
Add a synergistic poorly performed
rendition in the style of Glen Gould's
Bach C-minor Prelude from *The Well-Tempered Clavier,*
backed by rhythmic hammers, water pipe drips, phonic emissions,
buzzing bees, trumpets, out-of-tune strings, sticks scraped against
wooden fences with intervening piglet whines. It's not so bad.
Not once, lying in that steel tube, is there temptation to press
the hand-held panic-button. My secret?   Prior to passage
through the portal, keep eyes shut tight. Savor the cadence
during pestle-pounding. When the tormentor
declares the performance over—
as a spent torpedo—
I depart the vault,
no longer
chaste.

True Beauty

In this land of augmented breasts,
lifted chins, botox lips, lipoed hips,
pasties and lycra stretch, where skin
and bone are cut to fit the fashion,
there is a dull self-absorption
with our human forms, our temples.
I'm not speaking of reconstructions
for cancer survivors, other afflictions.

So I took my inherited wealth,
catered to my truth, styled my hair,
dieted a bit, got foxy new rags.

Then settled with myself, I sat
with Frost, Dickinson, and Bishop.
That's when I noticed the photo
across the room. Grandmamma
in crowning silver braids, high
Sicilian cheekbones, mellowed
Mona Lisa smile, speaks to me
of truths I have yet to know.

Sicilian Ceremony

Whaahuuu . . . whaahuuu . . . the breathy Marilyn
Monroe whistle of the Catania train as we slip
from sea, tunnel through mountains into
the heart of Sicily. My nephew, Max,
and his intended, Charlotte, resolved
to marry in the pink village where
his great-grandparents
grew and wed.

Three hours before we arrive at the tiny station.
Carlo, son of Pietro—Lord of San Giovannello Farm,
greets us. No bustling Taormina resort—this more mythical,
with a wheat-heavy valley encircled by verdant dotted
slopes of olive and almond groves. In jointly broken
dialects of language-limited tourists and natives, Carlo tells
of silent salt mines, lost livelihoods, as we cling
to jeep over dusty canted roads.

Just as twisted island byways, events turn.
Wedding delayed a day, venue change from cathedral
to public offices. The mayor, decked in green-white-red
ribbon sash, officiates. We cannot translate the cleric's
lilting lyrics as he addresses the couple. We smile,
applaud at the finish, raise flutes in naïve celebration.

Paparazzi-like reporters and photographers flit about
at the ceremony and reception. Champagne toasts,
Carlo's warm crusted bread, virgin olive oil,
antipasto piled high, platters plentiful with pastas,
sundry meats, cream-frosted cake, then Sicilian folk
dancing until the Grand Finale—band with mandolins,
zither, mouth bows, hand-clapping guests, all noisily
escort the wedding pair up the hill, to the matrimonial room.
We sing a midnight serenade beneath their soon shuttered window,
till a tell-tale sheet, shaken out the reopened sash.

Invitati da mezzo mondo a Villarosa
ma un certificato impedisce le nozze
reads the page one headline the morning after
in the Enna portion of *Giornale Di Sicilia*. We scan
the full pages, colored photos, joyously recount
the past day. Italian language-challenged—
unaware of printed details.

Not until our return to the States did the newspaper
translation reveal our innocent revelries. Something
about guests from halfway around the world,
wedding impeded for lack of the bride's baptismal
document. Bishop entreated to make exception—
He was steadfast—*no certificato, no nozze*.
Compromises made, ceremony enabled, a priest
scolded in Italian. "If I can bless a car, I can bless
your rings, but never attempt to marry in the church
without the requisite certificate."

Kisses and "abbracciares" abound before the fledging
couple climb into the Toyota four-wheel-drive.

Alone, I ascend a hill to find Villarosa keepsakes . . .
ke-ke-koo . . . ke-ke-koo . . . sotto voce clucking
of brown hens heard round the bend on my hunt
for red-hued granite stones . . . clinco-clinco . . .
clinco-clinco . . . call bells on sheep that peek
over the hill to see who approaches.
They lose interest, slowly back down.

We wake in damp aroma, to raindrops' tap, tap dance
on the stone deck of our Bella Vista lodge, the one grey
day of our stay. Pietro's wife, Marcella, notes,

"Villarosa weeps at your leaving." Tap, tap . . . tap, tap . . .
showers shift to a feather-mist on my face . . .
clinco-clinco . . . clinco-clinco . . . ke-ke-koo . . . ke-kekoo . . .
whaahuuu . . . whaahuuu . . . whaahuuu. . . .

. . .

Max and Charlotte, like Manzoni's doomed
lovers, Renzo and Lucia, hindered by Italian
religious form. We chuckle at poetic justice,
know Max and Charlotte's triumph—married
in the Town Hall, just as great-grandparents
Marianna and Angelo long ago signed
their nuptial papers before passage
to Pennsylvania mines.

Beneath the Rowan Tree

I drank a pint of stout with my dead dad
in Sligo's McGlynn's last night. He was singing
with the boys just like he did when I was a tot.
He could do bawdy tunes with his brothers
on Saturday nights, and on Sunday mornings,
tenor hymns. He never saw this land of his father's—
never saw much of his father either. A lone boy,
he drank milk fresh from cows on the farm
where he boarded. He told of new cowpies
warming his bare boy's feet
on frosty winter mornings.

This may be why when in the company
of these critters, I crow. Mellow cows
and their noble beaus, bulls, gentle in courtship—
the cow always wills *when.* Their young
dart about with eyes big, new to the outdoors.
Cows give wet kisses, warm milk rhythmically
streamed to stainless steel pails. It is their bad fortune
to be unable to bat flies from their eyes or scratch
their behinds in the field, unless near to a rowan tree.
Though common, they are *Irish,* these Joycean
silky kine—innocent nannies to humankind.

My dad did not *cast a cold eye . . . on death.*
I promised him my ashes, also, would be sprinkled,
with wind, warbler, and buzzing bee, beneath
the rowan tree, in view of a grazing cow or two.

Cooking Cream of Wheat

Silk milk swirls, stove light
glows gold and ice-blue
on waves the sheen of new
snow. With heat beneath,
a sweet smell rises. Foam
breaks out as alabaster
grains mix to thick

drifting memories. I see you,
flirting flapper, in the tarnished
silver frame. You were the eldest,
left coveted classes to help when
your father could no longer climb
into that bituminous pit. I saw
you sublimely posed
in another frame beside
your white-trousered groom.
You wrung clothes with the old
Maytag, after work, in the cellar,
in the night. You washed stains

of my pubescent embarrassment,
said when sex was best,
thought yourself *big-boned,*
became bent, shrunk. That night
you woke in fright . . . *It's okay, it's me . . .
I'm your daughter.* You, who could play
a saxophone, balance books, stretch
a ground beef pound like loaves and fishes.
Here now . . . cooking cream of wheat.

Hummingbird

—for Susan

Hush . . . hear that . . . sort of a buzz-trill . . .
yes, it's a wing-whistle. Quick, look there,
at the pink hibiscus . . . a tiny dynamo defies
all laws of proportions. We didn't have much,
but we had hummingbirds out back.

It seemed huge—our yard in the yellowed album.
She four, me ten, on the lawn sunning in our underpants.
In another photo, my sister rides her trike
beside Dad and Gran till Sunday roast is ready.
After, we'd sit near as the folks told family tales—
the cousin who ran off without her kids,
uncle back from war, at the family picnic, caught
kissing someone not his wife.

These titillating tales, seeds to my sister's reflective
nature. She fully-fledged into mother, then
successful author. Like Ceres, she's goddess
of motherly love, sowing and reaping grain crops—
fits with the health foods she feeds her family.
She, always there for us, mostly me. Me mostly away.
Me more Juno, the bossy one, like itchy ivy
on the tree of life.

Through whatever mysterious grace, I embrace
this gift—my hummingbird sister.

Dulcet Laughter

for Eve

A resonant laugh over the phone,
her response to our sappy

Happy Birthday duet
to mark her new decade.

This splendid sound, similar
to his—more violin than viola.
Grafted to my family tree
that day her father and I

married, she is in my life
longer now than the years

I had with him. Her laugh
like a lyric poem

sweetens
lingering grief.

My Cousin Harmonia

for Ruth

If someone came up to you and said "Hey,
I'm your third cousin twice removed," who
would she be? A cousin is a cousin
to me. If pushed, I'll go so far as to
say the cousins with whom I grew up
were my first. I seldom see them. They're
removed—not in the mathematic
way of genealogy—scattered
now we're grown. All the same,

I love them. With an easy nod to kin—
the valid titles: *kissing cousin,
in-law, step, honorary, removed,
first, second, great, god*—I am not
distressed by these distinctions.
I assume love goes forward

and backward. I've learned my cousin has
been on an aching quest to find her birth-
mother, see resemblance in another,
to know what might be secreted in her
genes. She found the lady, learned
heredity. Yet this woman—who later married
my cousin's birth father—and a full-blood
younger sister denied my cousin

tenderness. How can I have been so blind
to her pain? I want to wrap my arms
around her, my cousin, this *Harmonia*.

Other Mother

Unable to bear my own brood,
I acquired, with each love, a daughter—
my family, not blended, is resolutely
mingled, like marble cake.

The first daughter but a child
when cautiously introduced.
Her lost dream—to rejoin parted
parents. Then, my husband—
her dad—died. We have shared
honeyed tea and nettled thorns.
We have recovered,
stepmother, stepdaughter.

The second, a grown woman
when we met, suffers wounds—
memories of mother mourned.
Her father and I see she plays
a child's tale of wicked queens
and tainted fruit. Still,
with wit we carry on.

Naked Echoes

7 AM
I slip out the townhouse door, dash
through drizzles, over puddles, to grab the *Times*.

>   I feel echoes of dawn's rain . . .
>   I hear echoes of past pain.

•••

We did the mild wild thing
last night. Not like early days when my body
was an orchestra for Tchaikovsky's "Pathetique"—
when it reached the third movement's brilliant climax—
when it made us late to parties—but rich as Bach's
Air on the G String . . . Matt's knowing hands.

•••

I hang his wet rain slicker in the hall.
Chilly in leather sandals *au naturel,*
unshackled, if a bit dotty. My husband
Matt fears a lawn man may pass by; still,
these parades through the place please him.

•••

I'd dreamed . . . something about Bush . . .
trying a new fish dish . . . the able hostess
morphed from Martha Stewart to needy
Norma-Jean—oh, I know this echo . . .
the getting lost scenario, frightened
I'd never find the way—from where

I can't recall—as the dream fades . . .
. . . starting sex anew after my husband
Rick took the overdose that widowed me.

Discerning dreams is like peeling
an artichoke, one leaf at a time.

· · ·

True luck, on a girlfriend-getaway some months
after the funeral, I met a decent sort, easy on the eyes,
widower, not complex but comfortable. He liked
country music—as had my Irish dad.
Me from Connecticut, he from Canada, we would meet
now and then in Nashville, waltz to Patsy Cline's
Sweet Dreams in the rain, under a white gazebo.
He implored; I said I wasn't the remarrying kind—
used him like Prozac.

· · ·

Passing the mirror, I meet my balding pube . . . hell,
this may be how old guys with thinning hairlines feel.

· · ·

7:30 AM
Most of my waking's, these days, begin
with unease. A weary Sisyphus until I step
into the shower, the baptismal spray often stirs
sudden insights. Eyes closed, I see clearly—
nascent poems, like unruly children,
begin to behave.

. . .

I towel off . . . hmm . . . not bad . . . down two pounds.
Matt brings coffee. I choose tan slacks,
a cream shirt from the closet, hear, from the garden,
a dove's coo-coo, coo-coo . . . I pause . . .
recall the doves of Knossos nearly 30 years past . . .
blind then to the Delphic Oracle's fated vision . . .

. . .

echoes that morning at the Cape. Rick stumbled
on the steps. The stroke—not the early Parkinson's—
slowed his speech, his thoughts, his witty aphorisms.
No more fast-finished-in-ink Sunday *New York Times*
crosswords. His mix-master phrases amused us—
okay, you be the nag-ivater, as we headed back
the next year. His torment a wave-drag on a sinking ship.
He took to writing lawyerly notes on the Corona—
like the last one left in the typewriter about extra cash
in checking, what a good wife I had been. . . .

    I learn echoes of silence . . .
    I contain echoes of absence.

. . .

I rebounded. How was it,
I have received such favor—two admirable
men of good humor . . . human foibles too.
Rick the fallen Elm, Matt the Red Maple
of my arboretum. My new groom's grace
when I called him by Rick's name—"That's all right,

I think I would have liked him." Ready-made families
come with both husbands . . . a cursing perhaps,
to be barren, but more a blessing—joy, love
without tricky kid-rearing skills.

I douse pale fleshy ends of artichoke leaves
in melted lemon butter, pull them dip side down
through teeth, over tongue, find the full flavor.

    . . .

8:15 AM
I head to the kitchen . . . the selva-like din
of a sudden burst outside . . . Uganda rain riffed
our tent in the night, before the climb . . .
hands gloved to grasp sharp vines,
it took ten minutes for wet to hit earth.
"I checked my pulse on the mountain,
ventricular tachycardia," Matt said
in his physician's voice, Oh damn,
I'd nearly killed him, urging that trip
to observe rare mountain gorillas. I found
it remarkable, first tourists to arrive—
the new regime just settled—and last
to safari before later climbers,
tortured, murdered by
Rwandan rebels.

    . . .

8:30 AM
I open yogurt, granola, pour simmering
water into the French press . . . smile as I recall
being told of my granddaughter's kindergarten

declaration to mates, "My grandmother
just loves gorillas."

• • •

From the kitchen radio I learn
a major Turner exhibit at the Met this summer
will include his oil on canvas, *Snowstorm* . . .
I recall that day Uncle Dan invited me to ride
in the snowplow's cab . . . those vast waving
angel wings—one each side—as he plowed through
titanic drifts on Bacheller Hill Road past the cemetery,
out of Cassadaga. It was a white wonder world
of mountains, peopled by flying snowflakes, human-like—
each with its unique sameness. Odd, how much I enjoy
the snowless sun-blessed south. We winter now
in Naples Florida, summer on Long Island's shore . . .

• • •

9 AM
Back in the bedroom, I pull bedding together,
throw soiled clothes into the hall laundry—
Big morning news item: Viagra may cause
blindness. "No, it's more likely to cause onanism,"
Matt suggests . . . I laugh . . . his scientific wit.
In the *library*—our code for the loo—I ponder
my place among over-ripe humanity, all condemned
to suffer the plague of the petard . . .
skim *The New Yorker* . . . *The City* . . . my pleasure, to meet
friends at the Algonquin for drinks at day's end.
Ever since I first saw the actress on Broadway
in *A Room of One's Own,* my fantasy,

to run into Helen Mirren. We'd talk
about Helen's work in northern Uganda
with Oxfam. Maybe have a drink together.
If I were a lesbian, Helen would be
the kind of woman I'd want. All these
effusions flow from my deepest core,
melt like crystals rolling off an iceberg,
its true fathoms known only to me,
shielded under those artichoke leaves—
my vague dysthymia . . . at times impulsive . . .

      I hold the echoes of my nature . . .
      I survive echoes as an anchor.

      . . .

my rare rage—I snapped amid
Rick's tragic affliction. As if a bee-swarm
sucked me of all honey, I raced mad
into that long-ago night, like a malevolent
murderous woman, I wanted, no, I craved
a stranger to attack, to warrant my wrath.
Hours later, contrite for my fierce
outburst at his helpless accident . . . broken
toilet tank he'd used to right himself—
god damn Parkinson's Disease—
I see him on soaked knees, struggling
to wipe a sea of water . . .

      . . .

after Rick's death, I sought solitude . . .
Mercy Center on the Sound, where Rick's
former colleague who left the law, took her vows,

offered a modest cell not occupied. I spent days
in silent retreat. I did not believe, would not accept
a God of anger and diminishment, yet chose to sit
through a morning Mass—fought to keep faith
with the power of love and enhancement.
I found curious comfort in the single cot tight
to the wall, the hard wood chair, the lamp's dim
light-cone spilled over the pine table, laconic
communal meals, the black birds that strolled
about the bench, by the sea, on which I sat—
Rick admired their lucent beauty, wily ways. . . .

>   I learn echoes of silence . . .
>   I contain echoes of absence.

. . .

9:30 AM
Rhapsody in Blue on the Caddy's radio
as I start the engine . . . I heard that music
from the lodge that night between semesters.
I was camp nurse . . . someone screamed,
"A boy has choked. He's not breathing!"
Airway cleared, mouth-to-mouth—
Heimlich not yet known—one hour before
sirens. The boy died. Alone on the dock
I sobbed.

. . .

9:45 AM
Whoa . . . slow down. Don't need more costly tickets
or another crash . . . the icy road that day Rick and I planned
to return from the holiday family visit, eager to get back . . .

four months before I did—two in hospital, two in rehab.
My mind speeds along with the sedan . . . last night's exquisite
solo violinist at the Phil . . . his raffish grin had the look
of an appealing pirate as he rhythmically bowed
into the Concerto's crest. In the second curtain call,
he singled out the oboist with auburn tresses—
acknowledged her flawless performance.
Does he travel the world alone; does he take
a wife, a lover, along? Perhaps he asked
the oboist to join him later. At intermission,
Matt bought a signed CD for me.

...

In the darkened auditorium the autographed album
of graduate school days echoed in my mind . . .
my date showed off Jascha Heifetz's handwritten
note on the album cover. I didn't know, then,
who Heifetz was. The idea of my companion
as a beau was promising—handsome, successful,
pedigreed. There really wasn't a spark . . .
my naïveté regarding Heifetz didn't help.

> I endure echoes of Sisyphus.
> I meet echoes of my bliss . . .

...

10 AM
I steer onto the ramp, raise the volume:
Two-year-old found drowned in his parent's pool . . .
my mind turns to my cousin Jill's toddler,
in flannel nightie, reaching over burning
Christmas candles. Jill and husband upstairs
preparing for festivities. Soon after, Jill's sister

found her own twelve-year-old daughter, in snow,
murdered. Dead now, the burned toddler,
the pre-teen, broken grandparents, both sisters. . . .

    •••

Sisters—my little sister and I were
the Rowan girls with our hair in curls,
became genuine friends when she began
college, and I, in grad school. My Italian mom
had four sisters. I loved these aunts. Why hadn't I invited
my favorite, Aunt Jo, to my first wedding? It was small,
only close family and friends. Mom was angry with Aunt Jo.
I felt a wimp . . . acceding to my mother's mean claim.
A precious diamond, my mother could cut. Still, I anguish,
feel shame—never gave apology. I battle to smooth
my hard-edged stone of inheritance—

    I confront echoes of my spirit . . .
    I bear them till certain exit.

    •••

10:25 AM
I slow speed to better hear NPR speaking
of condiments . . . cilantro/coriander, vanilla—
seems vanilla is from the orchid family, derived from Latin
testes—yes, so like an orchid, to partner with vanilla.
Back to seasonings . . . saffron, Cleopatra's favorite
aphrodisiac. Cleo bathed in it to prepare her loins
for love. Saffron, exotic, tiny spice-threads hand-picked
from a crocus flower, warm fire but too much
can be like iodine. Moreover, saffron averts depression—

perhaps a diet of the tiny orange stigma will still
my moody nature. Beware of the Persians,
they do seduce you with saffron potions.

. . .

This talk of Persia reminds me of the clerk, Raschia,
who explained her name—a Persian virgin princess . . .
names . . . can be awkward things . . .
I never liked mine. It wasn't so bad, when
Miss Swanson, my favorite first-grade teacher,
used my nickname . . . about the same time
my playmate's granddad . . .

. . .

a matchstick stack of stifled reflection tumbles . . .
the shade lifts . . . I look through a lace veil . . .
her grandfather sat us
on his knees,
read stories,
took us
to the sink,
"peed funny"
into the bowl . . .
told us
not to tell.

Mercifully, that artichoke-thorn never
acquired the status of a "center choke."

. . .

11:30 AM
Oh *merde,* missed the exit. Might as well
go to the mall first. I'll pick up the *Don Carlos*
tickets on the way back, do groceries
after lunch. That will leave time to find
a gift for my granddaughter's birthday.
This spirited girl, about to date. I wonder,
with all the sexual freedom, will these kids know
the thrill of trespass . . . my first love . . . poor guy,
necking in the hall, holding me so tight.
Plaid pleated skirt, wool slacks—slim barriers
to his persistent teen boy-bulge. I asked
at the alumnae lunch a while back, "Was he
at the reunion? Dead . . . how long?" I checked
hometown obits. The site went back only three years . . .
zero. Tempted then to stop coloring my hair,
sanity retuned—back to blond . . .

· · ·

12 NOON
Tickets take more time than expected. Late
for lunch with friends—all writers—they forgive.
I promise myself to quit this bratty
tendency to be tardy. Lentil soup and salad
then on my way. First a high-test fill-up,
stop at the market. Artichokes look great.
I pick two. Consider time it takes to steam them,
make their thorny leaves fleshy, thistly sharp hearts
tender. These plants, knights in armor,
prepared to protect parts in peril.

· · ·

3:30 PM
Matt, home from golf, helps fold socks, remarks
on the brown one I unwittingly bleached tan.
I feel a flirtatious girl, choose smart black
pin-striped slacks, black V-neck tee, casually tied
with a black and silver belt, white grey-striped shirt—
sleeves rolled just enough to cover aging elbows—
then snatch a snooze before the party.

    ...

5 PM
The phone . . .
it's Jan. Best friends, we've lately been calling
over martinis . . . talk of his asthma, her headaches,
his prostate, what the President did this time,
how was Santa Fe, can we manage to meet
before fall . . . forty-some years, yet again
we crack up recalling the lamp cord I tripped
over in that tawdry Islamorada motel, on the way
to Key West in the rented red convertible . . .
met those two . . . My friends complete my arboretum—
persimmon, ironwood, balsa . . . Jan, the teak timber.

    I reap echoes of love. I embrace . . .
    I seek to generate love with grace.

    ...

10 PM
We leave the affair later than planned. This night—
my middle back in a mild migraine-like pain—
I anticipate cool sheets. An encore shower
unties knots in my spine. Memories cloud around me . . .

really re-memories. Nothing remains the same
in the rememberings . . . sadnesses, madnesses, stings,
exhilarations, fears—a cascade of failures
with family, with friends. My mingled kin,
drawn together by love—amorous and kindred—
fated to part, by broken expectations, by death.
Memories, like stars, endure and—contrary
to the cosmos—brighten in the re-remembering.

• • •

So, as with artichokes, I cautiously
peel off the sheath of leaves, gently
pull away the choke
to savor the center.
An imperfect process—
this getting to the heart.

> I face floodlights and shadows . . .
> I carry a coat of endless echoes.

• • •

10:45 PM
Out of the shower, nearly dry, I blot
the glistening beads that thread down
my easing form with the wrung cloth.
I stretch, hungry for sleep, fall into bed
beside Matt, keep the paperback closed—
Poe pointless for tonight . . . a crack of echo
breaks in my brain—it wasn't Helen.
A Room of One's Own starred Eileen
Atkins, not Helen. There would be no

sharing Uganda memories. I forgive
this breach, as there is eerie resemblance—
both Brits, with genius to act
the women of O'Neill and Woolf.

...

11 PM
In my somnolent state, I begin to plan
my own memorial. First, my ashes will be boxed,
ready for sprinkling. Family and pals might read
from my "collected poems"—well, it could happen,
there is an encouraging editor or two.

...

Then a flute or more of Prosecco,
easy to hold croustades—topped with
crème fraiche and Caspian Sea caviar.
And mixed fruit with sturdy picks . . .
and madeleines . . .
of course, Gran's Italian Pizzelles . . .
had I really seen Gran—bloody
hatchet in hand—chase the headless chicken
we would soon eat, around the yard,
near the goat pen, next to Gran's squash?
Or was it a tale? My five-year-old eyes
saw a real garter snake on the hill by Gran's
home where we lived while my dad
was on strike from the factory . . . Gran's fresh
sugar-bread and milky-junket were the best.

...

Perhaps I will try the memorial menu
at my approaching birthday gala . . .
damn . . . I'll miss wrapping my lips
around the risible "sex-agenarian"—
my pet self-identity.

> I confront echoes of my spirit . . .
> Yes, I bear them till certain exit.

   . . .

11:30 PM
So, to the memorial music . . . enchanted that evening,
my tears spilled into sweat of the steaming
August chamber performance at Music Mountain . . .
yes, there must be the same Dvorak String Quintet . . .
yes the one in G major . . . pity I must miss it . . .
yes, Patsy Cline's *Crazy, Sweet Dreams* . . .
surely Bach's *Air on the G String* . . .
amused at the thought of my fizzling
naked body under the slicker this morning,
I lust for vanilla junket. I'll find a recipe
tomorrow . . . know I'll wake
to the grim gnawing
ache of age . . .

   . . .

Is my future behind me?
No . . . *frailty* is not this woman's name.
Dark musings will not dominate my life.
Yet, like Sisyphus, it is tricky
to *nag-ivate* this absurd road . . .

I know echoes of my story . . .
I know echoes of my glory.

When You Don't See What's in Front of You

*Image of Louise Bourgeois with her latex piece "Fillette" (1968)
by Robert Mapplethorpe*

In white and black,
Louise Bourgeois sits
before Mapplethorpe's camera
with a glint in her eye, aware
he might create a controversial
photo. She cradles her carving
(an immense common carp?)
from the crook of her right arm
to her hand. Her little-girl grin
prepared to face her future.
I admire her mellow
knowing smile.

Oh,

on second sight, with
brighter light, I see
beyond her elbow,
discover she grasps,
a fish of a different sort—
the thing a codpiece
confines. I consider
her character anew.
Clear now, she delights
in blissful tumescence.

The Greek Ring

The petit ring vanished,
I thought it forever gone.

As I shake away the dust,
from his shoes,

I feel myself return
to that noon escape

from sultry sun—
his nectar comes to me now.

After,
we sipped ouzo,

strolled the Plaka,
chose the golden ring.

Three winters pass
in my widow's bed.

Finally, I take away his things,
leave snow gear till last.

My light,
a blush of gold

from an upturned boot,
the ring tumbles.

Something about Sligo

> "This Summer School changes lives . . . some things happen nowhere else but here."
> —Prof. Meg Harper, U. of Limerick,
> Dir, 56th Yeats International Summer Sch. Sligo, IE, 2015

Sligo's secret manifested during my stay
in Ireland's northwest coast town. Someone said
a summer-school student challenged the curse—
stole a stone from bloodthirsty Queen Medb's
grave-cairn atop Knocknarea. On the return,
he fell down the steep slope, broke his right
writer's wrist. No doubt, the Sidhe—
other-worldly beings, fairies—benign
unless angered by a mortal's foolish deed.

All twenty-six of Yeats's plays were performed
this Sligo week, many alfresco, to celebrate
his one-hundred-fiftieth. As I watched,
The Land of Heart's Desire made real
when the performance dramatized the clash
of pagan and Christian values—

> *Who goes with them must drive through the same storm . . .*
> *the hurtling foam . . . The wind blows out of the gates*
> *of the day; the wind blows over the lonely of heart . . .*

At that moment, raw wet winds erupted, roared
and waves crested. crashed onto Rosses Point strand
as the innocent bride of the play was lured away.

Not to worry, for Sligo town rests between
Yeats's *bare Ben Bulben's head* and Knocknarea—
with big-shouldered bearing, these buttes magically
protect the enchanted valley they embrace. Yes,
some things happen nowhere else but here.

Favors from Fierce Seas

What I seek on a beach—
shells, shards, a host of stones,
often ignored or overlooked by those
centered on a plunge into the sea.

Here, green glass gems; there, a spiral
conch shell—hold it to my ear and hear
an ocean of tones that call forth home,
a shore of sunrises, sunsets, storms.

Swans sail by, gulls face stiff winds,
monarchs breed on near milkweed,
binge on butterfly bushes to prepare
for the journey before them.

I gather assorted wave-tamed
pebbles—my preferred fits
betwixt thumb and fingers
as I feel favored features—

incised wounds once sharp,
now sanded to nuanced solace.

Clear West

When the air is right clear here
    I hear gulls of Galway Bay.
        When I let my eyes' curtains

        slip low, I see seabirds sail
            over Moher Cliffs. I see them
                stand, like centurions, face
    to wind. I see them cruise
        over Dingle's castles, as mist
            moves through mountain passes,
  settles in cradles of Connor's
    crevasses, until hard rain gathers,
        grows mountain rivers, driven
            to descend in cymbal crashes
                of Beethoven symphonies.
  I see seagulls glide over stone-
    boxed meadows where a confetti
        of sheep slow dance in soft rain
            to rhythm of chomp, chomp-chomp.

When the air is right clear here,
    this is what I hear,
        this is what I see
            to the east from
                my wood deck
                    overlook on
                        Long Island Sound.

III. The Spur to Persist and Thrive

I thought:
maybe death
isn't darkness, after all,
but so much light
wrapping itself around us . . .
      —Mary Oliver, *Owls and Other Fantasies*

"Go back?" he thought. "No good at all! Go sideways? Impossible!
Go forward? Only thing to do! On we go!"
      —J.R.R. Tolkien, *The Hobbit*

. . . the best way out is always through.
      —Robert Frost, *A Servant to Servants*

For My Husband in Equatorial Africa

When we stood before grown
children, old friends, family,
vowed to keep this love
found between twin sorrows,

did you know you would one day
be by my side soaring the Sahara,
to Entebbe where trigger-happy
travelers now shoot photos?

We, two silver-haired creatures, would
trek the Impenetrable Rain Forest,
climb to rhythmic machetes where
dense jungle fills hungry air . . .

steep, steamy hours . . . lungs breaking
mud legs aching . . . higher . . . hush . . .
they were close . . . a bush moved . . .
we heard thump-thump, then . . .

we saw the sleepy "silverback"
and his mellow mountain family.
No more, aware of breathless air . . .
we twelve, six human, six gorilla.

Bliss, to reach the base, camp
showers, a fine wine by night's fire,
sublime conversing with our mates,
tropic rain patting a tented top.

My world is now wide
once more; my love for you
is larger than this glowing
golden land of Africa.

Time Now

Time now
to grind coffee beans for our French Press
to notice the top of the toothpaste tube needs
      your flattening squeeze
to swear without annoying you, you who never swore
      in all our years together
to lay my arm across the empty pillow by my side
to find on my own, my often-lost phone
to miss heating my chilled fingers under your warmth
      beside me in bed
to avow the wisdom of the raven who settled
      outside our window this spring,
      days before we learned your diagnosis

Time now
to marvel at the cartful of children, stepchildren,
      and grandchildren we've amassed
to look stuff up, instead of asking you
to ponder how the pleasure of your rationality, tempered
      your contrarian nature
to savor the last frozen slice of your home-baked French bread
to pump my own gas
to consider your integrity when you refused a friend's advice
      to purchase a particular stock on insider information
to reflect on how I nearly killed you, trekking mountain gorillas,
      on those merciless Ugandan Virunga Mountains
to choose which of your shirts to sleep in this night
to rejoice in how blessed I am to have loved you, you gentle-man

Time now
to treasure your last gift, as I told you of my love
      when your eyes opened to meet mine in a final embrace

What's the Point?

The feather
given me
has no point.

My folio would
be filled in blunt
forms, if not for

my choice to seize
the quill, sharpen
its hard hollow nib,

pursue the gift
with passion,
compose this poem.

What's Next

Wildfires ravage
Aspens sprout

Oceans roil
Seas settle

Clouds burst
Sunbeams embrace

People perish
Babes birthed

Loves lost
Memories remain

We halt
We resume

Cadences

for Michael, Marlene, Eve, David

This time, it was my loved husband.
Soon after a dear pet, put down.
Our good friend who often joked
in past years, "I'm shipping out
in the morning," stroked,
and did just that.

It began when my first wedded
chose to end his disease, before
it ended him. Three months later,
my dad died. At the vet's the next
month, my funny Frenchie breathed
her last slight snort. . . . Took years
before the silk thread stopped
spinning; the cocoon formed,
evolved to a hard shell. I emerged,
flapped my wings, began to fly.
A butterfly then.

Still, with love, of pals, of kin—
step, in-law, grand, and great—
this cadence sustains me.
A silk moth, now,
I cede the certain center,
the ever-constant chrysalis.

The Men I Married

for Joe and for Gerry

To those who know me well
This will come as no surprise.
To you, here is what I'll tell—two
bright guys, with tight thighs.

IV. My Menagerie

"Hope" is the thing with feathers—
That perches in the soul—
And sings the tune without the words—
And never stops—at all—

And sweetest—in the Gale—is heard—
And sore must be the storm—
That could abash the little Bird—
That kept so many warm—
    —Emily Dickenson

Hang on to your hat. Hang on to your hope. And wind the clock, for tomorrow is another day.
    —E.B White, The Letters of E.B. White

Imperial Grace

Scarves of monarch butterflies flurry
over marsh and hemlock milkweed walls
to break fast without care or hurry
among neighboring boisterous sea gulls.

Valiant migrants of the nation's margins
flit in slight vapors of *Caesar's last breath,*
move through Maine to Mexico mountains—
there, call a consort to mate before death.

Hear waves of rustling silk as they rise
like delicate blankets from boughs bent
on fir trees that reach to sunlit skies—
a blaze of red-orange wings swirls in flight.

Behold these brief beings and realize
we gaze on cosmic flames of paradise.

Backyard Dominion

We have a *husk of hares* keeping house
beneath the spruce. A *murder of crows* cries
curtains to a cruise of caterpillars.
A paparazzi of flies flitter
about a minuet of deer. Meanwhile

the *charm of finches* enchants a *knot
of toads*—or are they princes? From this place
to Africa camp where a handsome
of warthogs flee a crush of hippos,
a sail of flamingos tack in the clouds.

As if a sentinel of topi, we watch
a mellow of gorillas munch potluck
and know, over all these and more,
we humble of humans are bound to keep
wise steward on this splendid sphere.

Food for Thought

She was heard to say she had to pick up
a million pigs this week. Just how does one
go about picking up a million pigs?
No matter how small, a million new-furrowed
piglets, at one and a half pounds each, will not
fit into her Chevy Suburban—picture
the weight of three thousand Sumo wrestlers
packed into five hundred Pontiac Sport
trucks. Can you imagine the racket?

Moreover, what does one do with a million pigs?
Pity the plight of unwanted pet pigs
without the Illinois "Pig Pals Sanctuary,"
home to the likes of Gert, Sadie, and Petunia.
More likely the usual fare of ribs, chops, roasts,
bacon, and, of course, tiny feet—pickled, stuffed,
or with jalapeno peppers—is planned
for her million pigs. Doubtful this woman
will fatten up her million porkers on the family farm.
Odds are, she'll take them to a hog factory

where piglets' ears are notched and their tails
cut off without anesthesia or pain relievers.
Sows and boars are confined in two-foot-wide
metal pens, sans straw—too expensive.

Does she know their moms prefer tidiness,
are smarter than most three-year-old tots?
Does she sleep well while assembly-line
fodder pigs live a nightmare
from breeding to slaughter?

What? You say she actually said
she had to pick up
". . . a million
things."

My New Live-In Pal

Chapter 1. December 2021

I met him in Philadelphia
six months after being widowed.
My Philly family knew him.
We clicked within minutes
of our being introduced.
On the train to Connecticut,
I kept thinking of his
dark dashing figure.

Days later, he appeared
at my door. Accompanied
by my very dear daughter-
in-law, who drove them
through jam-packed
Manhattan to Hamden.

Though there is need for caution
after such a fleeting courtship,
he is a bit slippery. Might be why
my granddaughter calls him "Butter."
I've always been attracted to bright
guys—and he is smart. Toilet trained
to the sandbox in a flash.

"Oh, Oma, you must take him"—
a gift—this charmer, a slim-hipped
hamster of Syrian descent,
perhaps out of a tunnel
in Aleppo.

Relocated now to a condo
with a private penthouse
in a corner of my sunroom.
I'm considering how best
to groom him for the future.
Should I register him now
for Andover? Definitely
not Choate, as only Yale
will do—well, I did say
he is quite clever.

Chapter 2. January 2022

So, lately, Butter's been hanging
out in the penthouse, avoiding me
except for my wee, carefully cut
carrot, apple, or broccoli treats.
Concerned he may be under
the weather, especially
as I've found little to clean
in his sandbox potty.

The first major condo-crate
cleaning caused a dreadful
shock. Prompted me to evict
him from the penthouse—
in fact, I removed it entirely.
So now my frustrated pal
spends time trying to trace
his old path to the penthouse.
A positive, as he gets plenty
exercise and keeps his slim
physique. Most pivotal, no
pooping in the penthouse.

A Fish Empathy Project?

Give me a break—the headline:
*Animal rights activists' campaign
pitches fish as smart and sensitive.*
They say fish should not be fished.

So what happens to the food chain?
Is it crueler to be hooked and cooked
than bumped-off and baked? No
moral person would deny needless
suffering inflicted on beings is wrong.

I know, I know, I can't really square this
with my little-girl goldfish and guppies,
but tofu chowder just doesn't delight
edacious desires. So, fish with nets that don't
unwittingly capture and kill unwanted sea
creatures—nets that will not sweep seas
absent of the species. Or go for a temporary
ban like the one on Gulf grouper fishing
that fosters future fish platters.

So, here we are, back
to the food chain—
think, *five loaves
and two fish.*

The Mourning Dove

the mourning dove sings
atop a weeping willow
I hear the high coo

Cost of Carnage

A keening echoed in my mind as I passed
the freshly severed giants lying roadside.
Their bare hearts exposed, spring's leaf-
budded branches cleaved off, trunks
wreathed in gray girths, left to weep.
Redolent of massive African Bush
Elephants, their tusks gouged out,
left to bleed a slow, torturous death.

What will life on earth be without
oak trees and elephants?

This morning a tiny spider joined me
in the shower. I considered ousting it
as it struggled to stay clear of water spray.
On drying down, resolved to rescue
the spider, I found it fallen
into a small water-drop,
drowned.

Unseen Peril

Gaze no more in the bitter glass.
—W.B. Yeats

The crash occurred in early
morning sunlight after a recurrent
night of tears. An added stun
to my new, young widowed role.
As years pass, that sudden thud,
when the House Sparrow crashed
into my window, still pains.

The thing about birds, they fly—
often into reflections of the world
about them. Yearly, billions of birds
wing into glass goliaths from Dubai
to Dublin. Whatever divinity
spawns this sublime perilous earth,
she has the wit to create avian derring-do
Black-tailed Godwits. These Icelanders
love to winter in Belfast Lough,
on rare occasions in Sligo Bay's
worm-rich mudflats, where cousin
Bar-tailed Godwits hang out till
weather warms. Unless, after
triumphant migrations of hundreds
to thousands of miles, they are

doomed to die in seconds on a pane
of ghostly glass. It's as if one pilots
a plane from New York to Paris but fails
to see the Eiffel Tower looming. I catch
my image in a mirror; reflect, what did
I not see, that night he took the overdose.

The Raven Reveals

When the world began the only colors
were white and black. I came, dressed
in richest of colors. Yet, I wished to look
like all others and became sad, so shook
and shook and shook my feathers
till all colors settled throughout this earth—
      a favor evermore.

I was left entirely black, but in sunlight
rich rainbow colors reflect off me. Some
disparage us. Perhaps they have yet to know
how admirable is our ebony? We are the black
piano keys that break the mold, blend the pitch
to bring blues style and jazz. Furthermore,
absent them it would be hopeless to find
one's place—you'd have to begin
again each time, counting life's
keyboard to find the proper note,
realize the right rubato.

I remind you Elijah was fed by ravens
while he hid from Ahab. Job tells us
Yahweh provides food for us and our young.
How lucky are we to know such favor. Naturally,
it was a raven Noah first sent from the ark
in search of dry land. We are a symbol of God's
providence. Of course, the Brits still depend
upon Celtic cousin raven—Bran the Blessed—
to keep their Tower safe. We traverse the heavens
and the earth with tidings, harsh and humane.
Need I cite all the world's raven fables to convince
we are curious clowns, cleverest of all birds?

We are not "nevermore" spouting spooks,
unfairly penned by that passion-pining
poet of macabre. We ravens do not prey—
for we are opportunivores who benefit
from blessings others snub. These are gifts,
        evermore favors.

Appreciate our mystique—our voices,
our whimsy, our alluring beauty. Trust
us, it'll make sadnesses less stinging,
help to discover joy, smiles, in the least
expected places. This wisdom,
        a favor evermore.

We forgive those ancient glossaries
that carelessly cast our collection—
in the huntsmen's terms of venery—
an *Unkindness of Ravens*. Unaware
were they of our true nature, our
forever honor. Know us,
        evermore.

Ecstasy

Once
        I held a newly healed raptor.

Placed in my palms,
long tail feathers drawn low,
the puff-feather form throbbed.
So too, my mortal pulse.

Once
        a wild hawk turned,

faced me with wide blazed
melon-yellow eyes. Held my gaze
in search of providence. She filled
my left glove as I eased grip
in a gentle *Tai Chi Spreading
the Eagle's Wings Movement.*

Once
        I loosed a Red Shouldered Hawk.

A chorus of scattered shrieks—
phoebes, terns, swallows—
warned of danger returned
to the aerie. Her life-mate soared,
spiral-dived in a sky-dance of courtship.
With wingspan wider than my open arms,
she lighted on a bare Slash Pine branch.
Her high-pitched *hear-hear-hear,*
a trumpet of liberty.

Once
        I felt a feather fly from me.

Notes

Bluebird, The Smith Sisters, Flying Fish Records: Lyrics appear in the poems "The Dead of Night" and "Black Birds Make Me Smile"

Italicized phrases in the poem "Backyard Dominion" are from *An Exaltation of Larks or The Venereal Game* by James Lipton, 1968

About the Author

Deanie Rowan LaPlante-Blank was born and bloomed near Chautauqua Institution, the internationally acclaimed arts community in upstate New York. Oldest of two daughters of first-generation parents—her mother, Carmella Rowan Conti, of Italian descent, and her father, Joseph George Rowan. Irish. She is an honors graduate of Public Health Nursing and Clinical Social Work from Syracuse University. Following her retirement as Director of a Community Mental Health Center in Connecticut and National Consultant with the Joint Commission on Accreditation of Health Care Organizations (JCAHO), Deanie began the serious pursuit of life as a poet. Her work appears in several literary journals and anthologies and has been set to music and performed. Deanie is a scholarship recipient from W.B. Yeats International Summer School in Sligo, Ireland.

Deanie Rowan LaPlante-Blank, mid this rich saga, ready for fresh ventures

www.ingramcontent.com/pod-product-compliance
Lightning Source LLC
Chambersburg PA
CBHW022145160426
43197CB00009B/1437